MODERN TRACTION PROFILES

THE
PRIVATISATION CLASSES

A PICTORIAL SURVEY OF **DIESEL AND ELECTRIC LOCOMOTIVES AND UNITS** SINCE 1994

MODERN TRACTION PROFILES

THE
PRIVATISATION
CLASSES

A PICTORIAL SURVEY OF **DIESEL AND ELECTRIC LOCOMOTIVES AND UNITS SINCE 1994**

David Cable

PEN & SWORD
TRANSPORT

First published in Great Britain in 2017 by
Pen & Sword Transport
An imprint of Pen & Sword Books Ltd
47 Church Street
Barnsley
South Yorkshire
S70 2AS

Printed and bound by Replika Press Pvt. Ltd.

Pen & Sword Books Ltd incorporates the imprints of Pen & Sword Archaeology, Atlas, Aviation, Battleground, Discovery, Family History, History, Maritime, Military, Naval, Politics, Railways, Select, Social History, Transport, True Crime, and Claymore Press, Frontline Books, Leo Cooper, Praetorian Press, Remember When, Seaforth Publishing and Wharncliffe.

For a complete list of Pen and Sword titles please contact
Pen and Sword Books Limited
47 Church Street, Barnsley, South Yorkshire, S70 2AS, England
E-mail: enquiries@pen-and-sword.co.uk
Website: www.pen-and-sword.co.uk

DAVID CABLE – OTHER PUBLICATIONS

Railfreight in Colour (for the modeller and historian)

BR Passenger Sectors in Colour (for the modeller and historian)

Lost Liveries of Privatisation in Colour (for the modeller and historian)

Hydraulics in the West

The Blue Diesel Era

Rails Across North America

Rails Across Australia

Rails Across Canada

Rails Across Europe - Northern & Western

Rails Across Europe - Eastern & Southern

Rails Across Britain

THE PRIVATISATION CLASSES

Introduction

Once upon a time …; but let us forget history because this book deals with the classes of locomotives and multiple units which have been introduced into the UK rail system since 1994 when the previous British railways were privatised. However, the sad part of the story is associated with the massive decline in manufacturing new rolling stock in the UK since that date, as we indicate below.

This book itemises the basic technical details of all the new classes introduced from 1994 up to the date of publication, with captioned photographs of each class in many cases showing different colour schemes and duties.

It may come as a surprise to some people to realise that the period between the start of privatisation to the present day, has exceeded both the BR Blue era and the Sectorisation phase. Indeed, the period is longer than that from nationalisation to the start of the Blue era.

The dearth of orders for new rolling stock in the later years of British Rail resulted in the new private passenger franchise operators inheriting some well-worn, increasingly unreliable equipment, and the freight operating companies fared no better. In order to convey a new image, and to meet the aspirations of an ever-increasing number of passengers in terms of speed, comfort and safety in an economically viable situation, the passenger franchises needed new train sets to be acquired.

Whether this has all been achieved, I leave the reader to decide. The freight operator's mixture of old and more recent designs also required much replacement as quickly as possible.

Manufacturing and Maintenance

In the days of British Rail, almost without exception rolling stock was manufactured in the UK, largely in the BREL (British Rail Engineering Ltd.) workshops. Sadly, we are left with only two companies – Bombardier and Hitachi – now producing multiple units, the facility at Washwood Heath used by Alstom for manufacturing having closed. Many items of rolling stock have been imported, not helped by the exigencies of the EU tendering procedures, which have not always helped British suppliers. Locomotives have been sourced from the USA, Canada and Spain, Multiple Units from Austria, Belgium, Germany, Italy and Japan, and wagons from France, Poland, etc.

Orders for new rolling stock are now placed via the ROSCOs (Rolling Stock Leasing Companies) formed under the privatisation act to take into account that rolling stock life was likely to be longer than the period of a franchise, so that at the end of a franchise there would be few complications in transferring the stock to a new operator, other than perhaps a change of colour scheme. Three ROSCOs were enabled – Angel Trains, Eversholt and Porterbrook – all of which have subsequently been bought out by banking groups and consortia.

In more recent times, smaller companies have leased rolling stock on a lesser scale from other sources. In the main, ROSCOs have the overall responsibility for their assets, but in most cases have sub-contracted maintenance on a day-to-day basis to the franchisees, or particularly for heavier work including overhauls to the few remaining workshops from BR days, now in private hands.

These workshops include the former BREL workshops at Crewe, Doncaster (Wabtec), Eastleigh (Arlington) and Wolverton, Brush Traction at Loughborough, plus a few minor locations such as Kilmarnock (Wabtec) and TMDs (traction maintenance depots) such as Selhurst, Neville Hill and Cardiff Canton. Contracts for new rolling stock now normally incorporate maintenance of the stock as part of the contract, resulting in the suppliers establishing designated sites for such work such as Northam (Southampton) for Siemens units of (SWT) South West Trains, Northampton for Siemens units on London Midland, Longsight for the Alstom Class 390s and Central Rivers for the Voyager DMUs. Three Bridges and Hornsey will service the new Thameslink Class 700s.

The New Classes

It is not surprising that in the last twenty years or so, a wide variety of new classes has been introduced; five new locomotive classes plus one major rebuild, and thirty-nine multiple units with two more in the pipeline. These are detailed below. Five manufacturers have dominated the situation, Electro Motive Division (ex-General Motors), Bombardier, Siemens, Alstom and Hitachi, with smaller incursions from General Electric and Vossloh. In many cases, standard European company designs have been adapted to suit the UK loading gauge.

The major rebuild was the stop-gap design Class 57, a re-engined higher horsepower unit with new traction motors housed in a Class 47 body shell, which was also improved for driver comfort. Although many Class 43 HST power cars were re-engined with MTU diesels, they were nothing like as comprehensively changed as were the Class 57s, and therefore do not count as a new class.

The book also includes two classes operated by Railtrack/Network Rail, which can be classed as trains, as compared with track maintenance equipment, which is outside the scope of this publication, as are wagons. These classes are the Multi Purpose Vehicles (MPVs), which are essentially load carrying units, primarily with tanks for railhead treatment and weed killing, but they have also undertaken experimental revenue work transporting containers. The other class is the Eurailscout, which although used for ultrasonic track testing work, was a high speed 2-car DMU, similar to the Network Rail HST set.

Let it not be thought that because all this multiple unit rolling stock was to new designs, it was trouble free. Retention toilets, when full, cut out of use, leaving passengers in difficulties. The 750-volt DC stock still has the old problems of 3rd-rail pick-up in snowy weather. Many franchise operators who specified what they wanted in the new classes, insisted upon cramped seating layouts with no relationship between seats and windows, minimal seat squab thicknesses and over-high seat backs, and never mind what the passenger wanted. The exigencies of safety impositions often result in delays to opening and closing doors, and air conditioning and some provisions for disabled persons add to the weight, requiring more power and associated cost. In many cases, air-conditioned stock lacks opening vents in case of failure.

However, on a more positive note, the units generally have superior acceleration than older classes, and sliding, rather than slam doors, are without doubt safer. Facilities for disabled persons are better than had been provided on older stock.

Generally, the new rolling stock is more reliable than the older BR commissioned stock. Depending on which of many bases of measurement is used, statistics indicate that a level of up to twice as reliable can be demonstrated. But this needs to be put into context, since the BR stock was getting older, and not replaced with new orders of up-to-date locomotives and units to the extent that has occurred since privatisation, especially once the new items had settled in after normal teething troubles, and with the new technology fitted such as on-board computer systems highlighting (potential) faults to the drivers and maintenance depots.

As mentioned above, suppliers are often contracted to carry out much maintenance as part of their contracts, and have a vested interest in demonstrating how good and reliable their equipment is. In this respect, the poor follow-up service from Alstom with their initially unreliable Juniper units, resulted in them losing out on the contracts for the replacement of slam door stock for South West Trains with Siemens units, which then achieved subsequent orders for units for London Midland as a follow-on. But now the Alstom Class 458s have been shown to be of a very high standard of reliability having had proper support allied to the excellent work carried out at SWTs Wimbledon depot. But Alstom's loss was Bombardier and Siemens gain.

Summary

This book has been produced to identify the different classes introduced since 1997 when the first new stock, the Chiltern Class 168s, were built, through the medium of a range of photographs, in the main taken by myself, and mostly unpublished. Other photos are credited as appropriate. It endeavours to give outline details, what they look like and on which systems they have operated, although this can be ever changing. The current colour schemes are illustrated, with some previous schemes, but a more comprehensive coverage of previous schemes is shown in *The Lost Liveries of Privatisation* published by Ian Allan Publishing Ltd. More detailed technical information can be seen on Colin Marsden's The Railway Centre web site, **www.railway-centre.com** and his *Traction Recognition* book also published by Ian Allan.

It will be noted that the great majority of the photos have been taken in the London and South East areas. There are two reasons for this. First, now that I am in my eighties, I don't travel away from home as much. Secondly, and more to the point, only six classes are not seen regularly in this area. They are Classes 139, 175, 185, 333, 334 and 380. Every other class can be seen in the south every day.

And if there is one thing above all about the Privatisation classes, it is the panoply of colours they have carried, so different from the days, thirty odd years ago, of BR corporate blue and grey.

David Cable
Hartley Wintney 2016

GENERAL CLASS DETAILS

This section gives an overall summary of the major elements of each class with a list of the relevant franchise operators. Full details of each class, including numbers, names and make up of multiple units with photographs can be viewed on The Railway Centre website and Colin Marsden's books *Rail Guide* and *Traction Recognition*. Full coverage of colour schemes can be seen from this volume and *Lost Liveries of Privatisation* by this author. These three books have all been published by Ian Allan Publishing Ltd.

Class Outline Details and Franchise Operators

57 Co-Co 120 ton locomotive with refurbished EMD 645 diesel engine and class 56 alternators. Rebuilt by Brush from class 47 locos. Class 57/0 and 57/6 engines produce 2500 HP, class 57/3 2750 HP. Maximum speeds 57/0 75 mph, 57/3 and 57/6 95 mph, the latter two sub-classes being also fitted with electric train heating supply. Used by Freightliner, DRS, Advenza, Virgin, Arriva Wales, Great Western, Porterbrook/West Coast Railways and Network Rail.

66 Co-Co 127-ton locomotive with EMD 710 diesel engine. Built by EMD, London, Ontario. Diesel engines of 3300 HP, sub-class 66/9 being low emission locos. 75 mph maximum speed, sub-class 66/6 regeared for 65 mph maximum. Body shell based on class 59. Used by EWS/DBS, Freightliner, DRS, GBRF/FGB, Colas, Fastline, Advenza. This class has also been used in Germany, France, Poland, Netherlands, Belgium, Norway, Sweden, Switzerland (Muttenz yards) and Egypt.

67 Bo-Bo 90-ton Locomotive with EMD 710 diesel engine. Built by sub-contractor Alstom at Valencia, Spain. 3200 HP with 125 mph maximum speed and fitted with electric train heating. Used by EWS/DBS, WS&MR/Chiltern Railways, Arriva Wales.

68 Bo-Bo 86-ton Locomotive with Caterpillar C175-16 diesel engine of 3750 HP output. Built by Vossloh at Valencia, Spain. 100 mph maximum speed, fitted with electric train heating. Used by DRS, with some locos sub-leased to Chiltern Railways and Scotrail.

70 'Powerhaul' Co-Co 129-ton locomotive built by General Electric, Erie, Pennsylvania, USA. Fitted with 3686 HP Jenbach, Austria diesel engine. 75 mph maximum speed. Used by Freightliner, Colas.

88 Dual-powered Bo-Bo Locomotive with 5360 HP 25kV electric output and Caterpillar C27 diesel engine of 940 HP. Built by Vossloh at Valencia, Spain. 100 mph maximum speed. Fitted with electric train heating. Used by DRS.

139 'Parry People Mover' 4-wheel bus-type bodied diesel unit with Ford 2-litre engine and flywheel to suuplement use of diesel engine. 45 mph maximum speed. Only 2 manufactured. Used by London Midland on Stourbridge branch.

168 3 and 4-car diesel multiple units (DMUs) with 422 HP MTU diesel engine per car. 100 mph maximum speed. Air conditioned. Built by Adtranz/Bombardier with Turbostar style bodywork. Used by Chiltern Railways.

170 2 and 3-car 'Turbostar' DMUs with 422 HP MTU diesel engine per car. 100 mph maximum speed. Air conditioned. Built by Adtranz/Bombardier. Used by Midland Mainline, Central Trains, Arriva Cross Country, Anglia Region, South West Trains, Hull Trains, First TransPennine, Scotrail, First Scotrail, Strathclyde PTE, Borders Rail, London Midland, Southern (for the Southern units also see class 171 below).

171 2 and 4-car 'Turbostar' DMUs as class 170, but fitted with Dellner couplings in place of the BSI type fitted to the class 170 in order to standardise with other Southern stock. Used by Southern.

172 2 and 3-car 'Turbostar' DMUs with 484 HP MTU diesel engine per car. 75/100 mph maximum speed. Built by Bombardier. Used by London Overground, Chiltern Railways, London Midland.

175 'Coradia' 2 and 3-car DMUs with 450 HP Cummins diesel engine per car. 100 mph maximum speed. Air conditioned. Built by Alstom, Birmingham. Used by First North Western, Arriva Wales.

180 'Adelante' 5-car DMUs with Cummins 750 HP diesel engine per car. 125 mph maximum speed. Air conditioned. Built by Alstom, Birmingham. Used by Great Western, East Coast (three sub-leased to Northern) First Hull Trains, Grand Central.

185 'Desiro' 3-car DMUs with Cummins 750 HP diesel engine per car. 100 mph maximum speed. Air conditioned. Built by Siemens, Germany. Used by First Trans Pennine. Arriva Northern.

220 'Voyager' 4-car DMUs with Cummins 750 HP diesel engine per car. 125 mph maximum speed. Air conditioned. Built by Bombardier in Belgium and UK. Used by Arriva Cross Country.

221 'Super Voyager' 5-car DMUs with Cummins 750 HP diesel engine per car. 125 mph maximum speed. Air conditioned. Fitted with tilting mechanism, although this has been de-commissioned on the Cross Country sets. Used by Virgin West Coast, Arriva Cross Country.

222 'Meridian' 4, 5 and 7-car DMUs with Cummins 750 HP diesel engine per car. 125 mph maximum speed. Air conditioned. Built by Bombardier, Belgium. N.B. These units were originally 4 and 9-car units, subsequently re-marshalled to 4, 5 and 7. Used by Midland Mainline, East Midlands Trains.

230 Ex London Underground District Line D 78 coaches, fitted with 2 Ford 3.2 litre diesel engines per coach. 2-or 3-car units with modified cabs and internal seating layout. 60 mph maximum speed. Built by Vivarail. Prototype DMU to be tested between Coventry and Nuneaton.

325 4 car Postal Electric Multiple Units (EMUs) with dual voltage power 25 KV AC/750 V DC. 4 GEC motors producing 1438 HP. 100 mph maximum speed. Built by Adtranz, Derby. Used by GBRF/FGB and later DRS on behalf of Royal Mail.

332 4-car EMUs with 4 25 KV AC Siemens motors giving 1877 HP. 100 mph maximum speed. Air conditioned. Built by Siemens, Germany and CAF, Spain. Used by Heathrow Express.

333 As class 332 with modified seating layout. Used by West Yorkshire PTE.

334 'Juniper' 3-car EMUs with 4 25 KV AC Alstom motors giving 1448 HP. 90 mph maximum speed. Pressure ventilated Built by Alstom, Birmingham. Used by Strathclyde PTE, First Scotrail.

345 'Aventra' 9-car EMUs fitted for 25KV AC. 90 mph maximum speed. Air conditioned. 380 HP motor per car. Regenerative braking. Built by Bombardier. To be used on Crossrail services (Elizabeth Line). This design will also be used for forthcoming London Overground services and those for Greater Anglia.

350 'Desiro' 4-car EMUs with dual voltage power 25 KV AC/750 V DC, with 4 Siemens motors producing 1341 HP. 100 mph maximum speed. Air conditioned. Built by Siemens, Germany. Used by Silverlink, London Midland.

357 'Electrostar' 4-car EMUs fitted for 25 KV AC. 6 Adtranz motors producing 2010 HP. 100 mph maximum speed. Air conditioned. Built by Adtranz/Bombardier. Used by LT&S lines.

360 'Desiro' 4 and 5-car EMUs fitted for 25 KV AC. 1341 HP. 100 mph maximum speed. Air conditioned. Built by Siemens, Austria and Germany. 4-car units used by Silverlink, London Midland; 5 car sets by Heathrow Express.

374 Velaro' 16-coach EMU developed from DB ICE sets. Built by Siemens at Krefeld for Eurostar services. 200 mph maximum speed, 21,000 HP power output. Dual voltage 25 KV AC and 1.5/3KV DC.

375 'Electrostar' 3 and 4-car EMUs. 3-car have 4 Adtranz motors giving 1341 HP; 4-car have 6 motors giving 2012 HP all with 750 V DC. 100 mph maximum speed. Air conditioned. Used by South Eastern, also by Southern before being refitted with Dellner couplings instead of Tightlock, thus becoming class 377.

376 'Electrostar' 5-car units with 8 Bombardier 750V DC motors producing 2682 HP. 75 mph maximum speed. Pressure ventilated. Built by Bombardier. Used by South Eastern.

377 As class 375 above. Sub-class 377-2 fitted for dual voltage 25KV AC and 750V DC Used by Southern, Thameslink, TSGN.

378 'Capitalstar' 4 and 5-car (originally 3-car) EMUs fitted for 25KV AC/750 V DC dual voltage (378-1 750V DC only). 6 Bombardier motors giving 2010 HP. 75 mph maximum speed. Air conditioned. Built by Bombardier. Used by London Overground.

379 'Electrostar' 4-car EMUs 25KVAC with 6 Bombardier motors producing 1609 HP. 100 mph maximum speed. Air conditioned. Built by Bombardier. Used on Cambridge and Stanstead Airport Services.

380 'Desiro' 3 and 4-car EMUs with 4 25 KV AC Siemens motors producing 1341 HP. 100 mph maximum speed. Air conditioned. Built by Siemens, Germany. Used by First Scotrail.

385 3 and 4 EMU's fitted for 25kv AC 100mph. Air conditioned. Built by Hitachi. To be used by Scotrail.

387 'Electrostar' units developed from class 379, but with higher maximum speed of 110 mph. To be used by TSGN, Great Western.

390 'Pendolino' 9 and 11-car tilting EMUs with 12 25 KV AC Alstom motors producing 6839 HP for 9 car units, 8793 HP for 11-car units. 140 mph maximum design speed, but restricted to 125 mph. Air conditioned. Built by Alstom, Birmingham and Alstom, Italy. Used by Virgin West Coast.

395 'Javelin' 6-car EMUs fitted for dual voltage 25 KV AC/750 V DC. 2253 HP. Maximum speeds - on HS1 140 mph, elsewhere 100 mph. Air conditioned. Built by Hitachi, Japan. Used by South Eastern.

444 'Desiro' 5-car EMUs with 750 V DC motors producing 2682 HP. Maximum speed 100 mph. Air conditioned. Built by Siemens, Germany. Used by South West Trains.

450 'Desiro' 4-car EMUs with 750 V DC motors producing 2682 HP. Maximum speed 100 mph. Air conditioned. Built by Siemens, Germany. Used by South West Trains.

458 'Juniper' 5-car EMUs with 750 V DC motors producing 2172 HP. Maximum speed 100 mph. Air conditioned. Built by Alstom. The former 4 car units have been augmented into 5 car sets using vehicles from class 460s which have been disbanded. Used by South West Trains.

460 'Juniper' 8-car EMUs with 10 750 V DC Alstom motors producing 3620 HP. Maximum speed 100 mph. Air conditioned. Built by Alstom. These units have all been withdrawn and the coaches modified and incorporated into class 458-5 5-car sets. Used by Gatwick Express.

700 8 and 12-car EMUs with dual voltage equipment for 25 KV AC/750 V DC power. 100 mph maximum speed. Air conditioned. Used by TSGN.

707 5-car EMU's of same design as Class 700. To be used by South West Trains.

717 6 car EMUs to be built by Siemens. 25 KV AC. to reokace Class 313 on Great Northern Metro services.

800 & 5 and 9-car IEP bi-mode and all-electric multiple units. 25
801 KV AC power with 938HP MTU. 801 Diesel engine for bi-mode working. 125 mph maximum speed. Air conditioned. Built by Hitachi in UK and Japan. To be used by Virgin East Coast and Great Western Railway.

MPV 2-car multi-purpose vehicles. Two 350 HP Railpac diesels per car (units have either one or two powered cars). 60/75 mph maximum speed. Built by Windhoff, Germany. Used by Railtrack/Network rail.

Eurailscout 2-car inspection unit used by Network Rail, now returned to Europe.

Note - The information regarding the makeup of units is correct at the time of writing, but is subject to change, for example such as class 390s having been originally 8-car units, subsequently becoming 9 and 11-cars. In addition, franchisees may have changed.

Other designs announced, but not yet introduced include: CAF 3 and 4-car EMUs, and 2 and 3-car DMUs for Arriva Northern.

Road traffic at Mount Pleasant comes to a halt once again, as the first Class 57, 57001 *Freightliner Pioneer*, accelerates away from the Northam curve with a Freightliner service from Southampton Maritime Container Terminal (MCT) to Lawley Street in May 2003.

57010 *Freightliner Crusader* heads north past Slindon in June 2000, on its way with a Freightliner from Southampton MCT to Crewe Basford Hall.

Before being marred by the Dellner coupling, Virgin 57311 *Parker* passes Headstone Lane in March 2004 at the head of a Euston to Manchester Piccadilly express.

The front end now disfigured by the Dellner coupling, Virgin 57308 *Tin Tin* leads the 4-coach Taunton to Cardiff service, with 57305 *John Tracy* tailing. The location is near Cogload Junction, and the date June 2010.

57311 *Parker* is seen again, this time at my local viewpoint, Potbridge. The train comprises three Silverlink Class 321 EMUs, being hauled from Bletchley to Eastleigh for refurbishment. Seen in August 2009.

Arriva Wales used four Class 57s for their Holyhead to Cardiff executive service, two in plain colours, and two as shown here. 57315 tails the return service in June 2010, carrying the company logo, and also showing the coupling in some detail.

A nice surprise was to find a pair of DRS Class 57s working the Bridgwater to Crewe nuclear flask service. 57009 and 57008 are passing Cam & Dursley Parkway in March 2010.

A Paddington to Cardiff Rugby special trundles along the down loop at Denchworth in October 2015. 57306 leads and 57310 in the latest livery brings up the rear.

The First Great Western Class 57s spend most of their time in darkness, since they are rostered to work the Paddington/Penzance sleepers. However, in mid-summer, a daylight shot can be taken as illustrated here. 57605 *Totnes Castle* backs the stock of sleeping cars from Long Rock to Penzance in June 2010.

A short-lived user of Class 57s was Advenza, whose 57005 rests at Cardiff with a display of Buddleia shrubs. June 2010.

Porterbrook commissioned a Class 57 to be built and in its somewhat garish colours, 57601 speeds past Lower Basildon in July 2001, working a Paddington to Plymouth express via Bristol. Note the two car-carrying coaches behind the loco.

57601 was subsequently sold to West Coast Railways, and in its new colours, is seen tailing a Scarborough to Windsor special passing Staines West in December 2006.

A pair of Network Rail Class 57s are seen at Potbridge on a murky day in February 2013. 57306 and 57305 are making their way from Eastleigh to Waterloo.

EWS 66130 heads away from the environs of Petersfield with the empty Fawley to Holybourne tanks in April 2006. This is a service now consigned to history.

The low January sun highlights the train against the dark background in 2006. 66076 passes Freshford with the Hayes to East Usk wagons in a nice mixture of colours.

An unusual activity for 66034 and 66162 was working an overhead wiring unit on HS1 at Tut Hill in July 2002.

EWS 66182 is seen approaching Churchdown with a trainload of matched army vehicles. The clouds portend an end to photography in October 2010.

The possibly unique combination of EWS 66184 and Wrexham & Shropshire 67014 *Thomas Telford* pass Battledown with a Hinksey to Eastleigh departmental service in September 2009. The 67 was seen on the following day at Gospel Oak working a container train from Dagenham to Wembley.

The coal dust swirls as 66202 speeds past New Barnetby with a westbound coal train in September 2004.

The regular morning Eastleigh to Hoo Junction departmental exceeds itself at Potbridge on this occasion as five EWS Class 66s are in charge of it. 66108, 66227, 66054, 66122 and 66200 do the honours this day in January 2009.

The Eastleigh to Hoo Junction departmental is seen this time at Farnborough Main with another interesting consist of 66078 towing 58033 and 58034. The latter were destined to work on the French TGV Est line, which was under construction. Taken in May 2009.

The classic view at Langstone Rock in July 2000, where 66015 passes with the Burngullow to Warrington China Clay tanks, watched by a variety of pedestrians.

EWS 66207 is ready to start away from Peak Forest in July 2016 with a stone train from Tunstead to Hope Street.

In DBS livery, 66152 pulls away from West Drayton with a train of box wagons for Acton. December 2011.

DBS 66152 has travelled a few miles since the last picture was taken. Working a departmental service from Doncaster to Tyne Yard, it is seen approaching Colton Junction in July 2016.

Beechbrook Farm was the site from which work trains journeyed whilst HS1 was being built, and which has now been restored to nature. Freightliner 66548 tails a trainload of ballast ready to leave the site in July 2002.

The author was asked by Freightliner Ltd to record a special train connected with naming one of its locomotives *P&O Nedlloyd Atlas*. The locomotive, 66532, heads a train of matched containers past Millbrook on a very short run between Southampton MCT and Millbrook Container Terminal. What a pity the September 2002 sun didn't shine on this ultra-clean train.

Freightliner 66551 passes South Kenton in September 2002 with a northbound train comprising a barrier coach and a Class 390 Pendolino.

66545 nears the summit at Ais Gill under the shadow of Wild Boar Fell in July 2009. The train is a loaded coal service from Ravenstruther to Ratcliffe-on-Soar power station.

In August 2005, Reading West was the base for self-discharge ballast trains on the Western region. Approaching Purley-on-Thames, 66519, with 66512 at the rear, head for Reading with a train from Appleford.

66520 heads east past Ruscombe in July 2007, with the empty cement tanks from Theale depot to Earles Sidings for Hope cement works.

It is all action at Ruscombe in August 2005. On the right, a First Great Western HST heads west; in the centre FGW 166208 works from Newbury to Paddington; on the left, what I came to photograph – 66560 with a diverted Cricklewood to Calvert Binliner. Closing speeds between the first two would have exceeded 200 mph, so my timing had to be spot on!

Trackwork on the North London line leads to diversions via the Tottenham & Hampstead route. Climbing up from below the bridge carrying the GE line to Enfield and Cheshunt, 66531 leads dead 90047 with a Crewe Basford Hall to Felixstowe intermodal through South Tottenham station. April 2010.

The first of the Freightliner Class 66s to be repainted into the Heavy Haul colour scheme, 66416, passes Ruscombe with a diverted Hams Hall to Southampton MCT service in March 2015.

A number of Class 66s have been given non-standard colour schemes. One of the first was Freightliner 66623 Bardon Aggregates, seen passing Denchworth in April 2007, making a nice change from the standard green.

66623 was seen a few days later working the Wool to Neasden sand train near Chalton on the Portsmouth direct line. This was an extremely rare diversion, to the extent that three loco hauled freight trains were seen in one hour, probably not equalled since steam worked passenger trains on this line in the 1930s.

Another colour variation was carried by 66522, with half the body carrying light green recognising the working relationship between Freightliner and the Shanks group. The loco is seen at Eastleigh in August 2005.

GBRF 66705 is seen standing outside Willesden shed (WN not 1A!) in May 2001, when these locos were serviced at that depot. The photo, which emphasises the length of these engines, was taken from a Gatwick Airport to Watford Junction Southern EMU.

Another of the loco-hauled trains at Chalton in April 2007 was GBRF 66717 *Good Old Boy*, which was heading south with the Mountfield to Southampton West Docks gypsum containers.

An amazing sight at Manor Farm Bridge, Cholsey, made even more amazing since I and my friend Ian Francis were the only two people on the bridge!!!! Now in First Group colours, FGB 66726 takes 87022, 87002 and 87028 from Wembley to Long Marston in January 2008.

FGB 66724 *Drax Power Station* passes Upper Holloway in April 2010 with a Grain to Ferme Park departmental service.

Displaying the Union flag, 66705 *Golden Jubilee* passes Harpenden in August 2003, making its way from Temple Mills to Croft with a train of ballast wagons.

Carrying a livery for the shipping line Medite, 66709 *Joseph Arnold Davies* heads a Felixstowe to Hams Hall intermodal service past Carpenders Park in May 2006.

Four locos were repainted to reflect the contract for GBRF carrying out work for London Underground Ltd. The striking Metronet scheme is highlighted in August 2007 by the late afternoon sun at Carpenders Park, where 66720 *Metronet Pathfinder* is hauling a Hams Hall to Felixstowe intermodal train.

Two of the locomotives carrying the Metronet colour scheme were repainted in conjunction with a naming ceremony associated with the 150th anniversary of the Underground. Carrying liveries reflecting London and the Underground system, they topped and tailed a special train working from and to Victoria via the Hounslow loop. In dull conditions in November 2013, 66721 *Harry Beck* leads the train past Wandsworth Town........

..........with **66718** *Sir Peter Hendry CBE* bringing up the rear.

66720 was selected to carry colours 'designed' by children, each side being different from the other. The loco is working a Bletchley to Eastleigh empty wagon train through Bramley in September 2011.

The last class 66 to be built was specially turned out to resemble the last steam loco built for BR. Named *Evening Star*, painted in Brunswick Green, with additional decorations, GBRF 66779 waits on the down through road at Doncaster in June 2016, with a train of sand from Middleton Towers to Monk Fryston.

GBRF acquired several Class 66s no longer needed by European countries. Most have been restored to the company's standard livery, but 66748 was still in a non-standard scheme in October 2015. It was seen at Denchworth that month, working the Westbury to Stud Farm departmental train.

Very much a stranger at the time, DRS 66409 creeps along the up main line at Millbrook to gain access to the container terminal with an intermodal service from Leeds. July 2004.

The state that locos working Rail Head Treatment Trains can get into is well illustrated by this working at Colchester in November 2010. DRS 66431 at the rear and 66432 at the front are working from Shenfield to Clacton.

Unusually on the down main line at Headstone Lane, DRS 66412 in Malcolm colours heads a Ripple Lane to Daventry service in September 2009.

The implementation of the Daventry to Grangemouth service on behalf of Tesco and Eddie Stobart provided for a special train to be run and loco to suit. In Stobart colours DRS 66411 *Eddie the Engine* passes Cathiron on the inaugural run in September 2006, with containers labelled 'Less CO2'.

DRS disposed of some of its first Class 66s, which were taken up by Freightliner, but retained the basic blue livery without inscriptions. Freightliner 66414 hurries through Colchester in September 2014 with a Felixstowe to Trafford Park service.

A Sunday Tesco intermodal from Mossend to Daventry passes Cinderbarrow, south of Oxenholme, in July 2016, behind class 66s 66434 and 66430, in the latest DRS livery.

Fastline had a contract to convey coal from Daw Mill Colliery to Ratcliffe-on-Soar power station. In its attractive colour scheme, 66305 heads north at Cossington with a loaded consist of matched GBRF wagons. September 2008.

A rather short-lived contract for Fastline was moving coal from Avonmouth to Ratcliffe power station. 66305 is seen again, this time at Denchworth in the same month.

Under threatening skies in July 2009 (so much for a summer's day!), Advenza 66841 passes Chesterfield with the empty steel scrap wagons from Cardiff to Stockton. The Advenza Class 66s were taken over by Colas.

Colas 66848 works hard pulling away from Wandsworth Road and is seen at Clapham High Street in September 2015. The train is the morning Eastleigh to Hoo Junction departmental, and was particularly heavy this day.

In its unique colour scheme to blend with the coaches of the *Royal Scotsman* tour train, 66746 brings up the rear of the train as it arrives from being serviced at Craigentinny, ready to proceed to Keith from Edinburgh in May 2016. The grey wording, *Royal Scotsman*, on the side of the loco does not show up at this angle.

Class 66s have also worked in several European countries, and a few examples are included here. HHPI (Heavy Haul Power International) 29002 passes Rotenburg (Wumme), Germany, with a Lahde to Minden coal train in June 2003.

HGK (Hafen & Guterverkehr Koln) DE61 passes Koln Sud with a northbound intermodal from Gremberg yard, also in June 2003 (and please excuse the lack of Umlauts!).

ERS (European Rail Shuttle Railways) PB07, carrying advertisements in the yellow band to recruit drivers, heads west through Tilburg, Netherlands, with an intermodal service from Germany to Rotterdam in May 2004.

Freightliner Poland has a substantial operation in that country, with locos in the standard green, with the exception of this. 66001 *Willy Brandt* pulls into Rzepin with a train of hoppers in August 2012. The striking livery can be seen in detail in the companion volume *Rails Across Europe – North & West*.

Last days of the loco-hauled mail trains in January 2004. 67026 has drawn to a halt at the old platform 9 at Reading with the Willesden Railnet to Swansea/Plymouth mail.

EWS 67008 crosses the causeway at Cockwood harbour with the Plymouth to Low Fell parcels service. The date is July 2000 and, needless to say, the tide is out!

Wales are playing at home in November 2006, so it is all action at Coedkernew. On the left 67023 heads towards Cardiff with a RugEx from Crewe, while on the right 50049 *Defiance*, heads a Newport to Cardiff shuttle service, 50031 *Hood* tailing.

67028 draws to a halt at Carlisle with the 'Northern Belle' from Aberdeen to Victoria in August 2005.

Although the Class 67s were obtained for mail services with 125 mph maximum speed, the cessation of the mail contract has left the class short of regular duties, resulting in them being used on some freight workings. An unusual one was when 67008 turned up on the Quidhampton to Eastleigh tanks in September 2003. It is seen at Campbell Road Bridge.

In the late afternoon in July 2006, 67013 and 67017 pass Manor Farm, Cholsey with the Avonmouth to Wembley Cargo vans, the sun providing some glint.

Major re-signalling at Basingstoke in April 2007, caused diversions of trains to Southampton via the Wylye valley. At Norton Bavant, a nice surprise for the assembled photographers was 67003 with a Hams Hall to Southampton West Docks intermodal service.

Another variety of duty for the EWS 67s was captured at Dean in April 2006, where a Serco test train was hauled by 67019.

Adding to the variety was 67016 passing Mortimer in February 2005, with Merseyrail 507030 which had been overhauled at Eastleigh, and was being returned to Birkenhead North depot.

The first Class 67 to carry DBS livery was 67018, seen having arrived at Cardiff with a train from Paignton in June 2010. The loco was named *Keith Heller* after the last CEO of EWS, a Canadian, thus being the reason for the maple leaf emblem.

Two Class 67s carry Royal Claret colours. 67005 *Queen's Messenger* is seen at Great Cheverell in February 2008, propelling the empty stock of a train from Old Oak Common to Westbury, from which it will form a RugEx to Cardiff.

Fortune sometimes favours the brave, as on this occasion when I had wandered down to my local haunt at Potbridge to see what was around. Without prior knowledge, the royal train appeared, led by 67005, with 67006 *Royal Sovereign* trailing. The train was being returned from Weymouth to Wolverton as empty stock in June 2009.

67029 carries silver colours, originally with the EWS three heads emblem, now DBS in a square. Named *Royal Diamond* and with the matching DVT leading, it is seen leaving Andover with the coach set used for VIPs, on its way to Marchwood on an overcast day in April 2008.

In 2012, to celebrate the Queen's Diamond Jubilee, 67026 was repainted and named accordingly. It is seen at Potbridge in April that year, with an empty stock train from Wembley to Eastleigh. Pity about the sixth coach ruining a matching set!

What was supposed to be the last train on the branch arrives at Folkestone Harbour. The Pullman train from Victoria is headed by 67029, un-named at that time. Seen in November 2006, with the tide out of course!

Arriva Wales replaced the Class 57s used on the executive Holyhead and Cardiff service with Class 67s. With a matched set, 67001 heads the morning service to Cardiff past Duffryn in June 2013.

When Wrexham & Shropshire Railways launched its premium service from Marylebone to Wrexham, it leased five Class 67s from EWS, which carried a silver/grey colour scheme. The three mark 3 coaches are tailed by 67014, which is seen leaving Marylebone for Wrexham in June 2008.

67012, *A Shropshire Lad*, passes Wembley Stadium on its way to Wrexham in August 2008, with the depot sidings full of Chiltern Class 168s.

W&SR 67014 *Thomas Telford* approaches the junction at Aynho in July 2010, making its way from Wrexham to Marylebone.

W&SR was taken over by Chiltern Railways and the locos lost the former company's name. 67013 *Dyfrbont Pontcysyllte* hurtles through West Ruislip on its way from Birmingham Moor Street to Marylebone in October 2011.

Chiltern Railways 67012, *A Shropshire Lad*, is seen again, now approaching Princes Risborough on its way to Birmingham in April 2013. The difference of gradient between the up and down lines to the summit near Saunderton is quite apparent.

DRS 68004 *Rapid* heads north near Normanton on Soar with a Mountsorrel to Crewe Basford Hall stone train in September 2015.

Chiltern Railways has leased some Class 68s from DRS. 68013 speeds through Northolt Park in April 2015, at the rear of a train from Birmingham Moor Street to Marylebone. As with the Class 67s, the loco carries the two-tone Chiltern colours.

With the well-known church at Kings Sutton in the background, 68014 heads towards its next stop at Banbury with a Marylebone to Birmingham Moor Street premium express in September 2015.

Instead of the normal Chiltern Railways liveried Class 68, DRS 68009 *Titan* puts in an appearance at Banbury in May 2016, working from Birmingham Moor Street to Marylebone.

A departmental service from Derby, topped and tailed by DRS 68004 *Rapid* and 68020 *Reliance*, enters Doncaster station in June 2016.

The ridiculous situation, caused by having removed run round loops and not converting enough driving trailers, results in two class 68s to work three coaches. Stabled at Norwich in September 2016, 68004 Rapid and 68024 Centaur will soon be ready to work to Yarmouth.

Two Class 68s have been leased to Scotrail. One of these, 68007 *Valiant*, has stopped at Dalmeny in May 2016, working from Glenrothes with Thornton back to Edinburgh.

Freightliner Heavy Haul 70003 passes Badgworth with a Rugeley to Stoke Gifford empty coal train in May 2010.

Class pioneer 70001 is in charge of a Felixstowe to Lawley Street Freightliner, seen at Carpenders Park in the late afternoon one day in August 2010.

70003 overtakes a Southern Class 377, as it makes its way between St Denys and Mount Pleasant with the daily Wentloog to Southampton MCT intermodal. It is photographed in February 2011.

The morning mist is starting to clear in March 2012. 70018 powers its way uphill from Reading to Basingstoke with a Birch Coppice to Southampton MCT Freightliner, and is seen near Silchester.

Framed between the tree and pole before the masts ruined the view at Lower Basildon, 70019 works a Southampton MCT to Birch Coppice Freightliner northwards along the Thames valley in March 2012.

70002 passes Hest Bank in May 2016 with a Daventry to Coatbridge service, with the branch from Morecambe about to merge into the down main line.

A close-up shot of Colas 70803, which is working the Westbury to Bescot departmental service, seen at Banbury in March 2014, with semaphore signal at attention!

Colas Class 66s were replaced on the Eastleigh to Hoo Junction departmental service by Class 70s, but have now reverted to Class 66s again. During the interim, 70809 was seen working the train at Potbridge in June 2014.

Colas sister locomotive 70804 works the same departmental service to Bescot, and is seen at Kings Sutton in July 2014, coming from cloud shadow into sunshine.

Due to motive power shortage at Freightliner, locomotives had to be borrowed from other sources. Hence, Colas 70808 was captured at Battledown with the Wentloog to Southampton MCT intermodal in August 2014 in less than sunny conditions.

Dual powered DRS 88002 hauls a test train of coal wagons at Velim in the Czech Republic in April 2016. (Quintus Vosman)

DMU 139002, a Parry People Mover, is one of the two units which work the branch from Stourbridge Junction to Stourbridge Town. It is seen at the Junction in February 2011.

Chiltern Class 168 DMU 168215 passes Wembley Stadium in August 2008, with a Birmingham Moor Street to Marylebone service. The end of the servicing depot is seen on the right-hand side.

Passing some track machines at West Ruislip, Chiltern DMU 168218 speeds through on its way from Marylebone to Birmingham Moor Street in May 2011.

Also seen at West Ruislip, 168106 heads towards Marylebone with a train from Birmingham Moor Street in October 2011.

Diverted from its normal route, Chiltern 168108 heads another unit and is seen near South Stoke on the Western Region, with a Birmingham Moor Street to Marylebone service in May 2002.

One of the original Class 168 DMUs, with the different cab to the Class 170 design used on the later Class 168s, 168002 draws to a halt at Banbury in February 2014. It is working from Marylebone to Birmingham Moor Street, and carries the new Chiltern Railways colours.

DMU 168215 passes South Ruislip with a Bicester North to Marylebone semi-fast service in April 2015. This train also carries the new colour scheme.

The franchisee for East Anglia introduced an innovative service between Colchester/Chelmsford and Basingstoke via the North London line, which, unfortunately, was withdrawn due to lack of custom and lengthy journey times. Anglia Turbostar 170203 is seen departing Farnborough Main on its way to Basingstoke in June 2000 with a service from Chelmsford.

An unusual sight at Brookmans Park was Anglia 170205 working a Hull to Kings Cross train in July 2002.

The Anglia franchise became the curious One group with its unique colour scheme. Demonstrating this in the low sunshine, 170202 passes Romford with a Liverpool Street to Lowestoft service in January 2008.

The Class 170s allocated to South West Trains have suffered transfers here and there – Northern Rail and now Chiltern Railways. In its pomp on SWT, 170306 starts away from Bramley with a train from Reading to Brighton in July 2001, a long-gone useful through service. In Chiltern service, they have been renumbered into a 168/3 series.

In the next incarnation, a former SWT Class 170 arrives at Huddersfield working a First Northern Rail train from Middlesbrough to Manchester Airport in July 2009. The pouring rain in the north is no match for the sunshine at Bramley!

Midland Mainline 170114 rushes down Sharnbrook bank and passes Souldrop with a Derby to St Pancras semi-fast service in September 2001.

Midland Mainline 170107 also works a Derby to St Pancras semi-fast, and is about to stop at Luton Airport Parkway in December 2002. These Midland Turbostars were transferred to Central Trains.

A Cardiff to Nottingham service operated by Central Trains arrives at Lydney in July 2003. The unit is 170516 in a pleasant colour scheme.

In less salubrious surroundings, Central Trains 170511 leaves Warrington Central in June 2000, working one of the long distance cross-country routes, in this case Liverpool to Norwich.

In 2005, Central Trains adopted a new colour scheme for its Turbostars, as demonstrated by 170112. The unit is seen at Undy in September of that year, working from Cardiff to Nottingham.

A few Turbostars carried advertising liveries. One such was 170399, a Porterbrook unit used by Central Trains. Displaying a colour scheme for the Derwent Valley, it is passing Magor in December 2005 on a Nottingham to Cardiff service.

170505 carried advertisements for Birmingham Bull Ring. Working from Gloucester to Nottingham, it was passing Churchdown in August 2004.

Another Porterbrook unit used by Central Trains was 170397 advertising Q-Jump. In a striking blue colour scheme, it passes Gatcombe on its way from Cardiff to Nottingham in January 2004. Pity about the yellow bag protecting the coupling.

The Central Trains Class 170s were subsumed into the Arriva Cross Country fleet, and in the new colours 170523 and 170639 are slowing to a halt at Badgworth outside Cheltenham. They are working another Cardiff to Nottingham service, the colours showing up very well in the March 2010 sunshine.

London Midland operates a mixture of 2 and 3-car Turbostars. One of the 3-car units 170 631 enters Droitwich Spa in February 2011 with a Birmingham New Street to Hereford train, passing the rather choice GWR bracket semaphore signal.

Hull Trains used Class 170s prior to employing Class 180s and Class 222 Meridians on their services. 170394 is seen at Harringay, negotiating the lines into Hornsey depot after travelling from Ilford in January 2005.

Southern acquired some Class 170s which were fitted with Tightlock couplings. These were replaced with Dellner couplings, and they were re-classified as Class 171s. In its original format, 170721 stops at Ashurst, working an East Croydon to Uckfield train in June 2004.

In Strathclyde PTE colours, but operated by First Scotrail, 170474 leaves Edinburgh Waverley with a service to Dunblane in September 2012. (Ian Francis)

With the Scottish Saltire showing its ownership, Scotrail 170450 leads a Glasgow Queen Street to Edinburgh service through the cutting south of Winchburgh tunnel in May 2016.

Displaying the colours of the new Borders Railway, 170414 starts away from Dalmeny station in May 2016 with a Glenrothes with Thornton to Edinburgh rush hour service.

Having exited the Forth Bridge, Scotrail 170394 speeds past Dalmeny with a Dundee to Edinburgh service on a Sunday afternoon in May 2016.

The Southern Class 171s are formed into 2-car and 4-car sets. 4-car 171803 hurries through Norwood Junction in August 2012, working an Uckfield to London Bridge service.

Another Uckfield to London Bridge train passes Honor Oak Park in July 2010, operated by Turbostar 171802. The 2-car sets are numbered in the 1717xx series.

Also classed as Turbostars, but with a modified front end, the Class 172s are formed into 2- and 3-car sets. London Overground 172005 pulls into Harringay Green Lane, with a Gospel Oak to Barking GOBLIN line service in August 2010.

Chiltern Railways 172104 passes the time of day at Marylebone in October 2011.

A pair of Chiltern 172s, 172102 in the lead, sweep through South Ruislip on their way from Marylebone to Stratford-upon-Avon in April 2015.

The semaphores at Abergele do their duty as First North Western Coradia Class 175 011 passes with a Holyhead to Crewe service in March 2004.

The Arriva colours do little to improve the design of Coradia 175009, which is seen at Duffryn whilst working a Manchester to Cardiff service in June 2009.

The Arriva colour scheme is seen in more detail on this 3-car Coradia set passing Coedkernew in March 2007. 175110 travels west towards Cardiff, having commenced its journey in Holyhead. The front end is somewhat lacking in appeal!

One of the First Great Western 125 mph Class 180s is seen at Churchdown in August 2004. 180109 is in charge of a Paddington to Worcester service via Gloucester.

In First Group colours, Hull Trains 180113 passes Alexandra Palace on its way from Kings Cross to Hull. It is overtaking a Class 313 on a Moorgate to Welwyn Garden City train in July 2010.

In Grand Central black and orange, 180112 speeds past Brookmans Park in April 2010 with an afternoon Kings Cross to Sunderland train. This is now a location where barriers prevent a photo in what were safe surroundings.

Storming through the smart station at Welwyn Garden City in July 2012, Grand Central 180114 is working a Kings Cross to Bradford service.

The Class 185 Desiros were only seen in the London area on delivery runs to the north of England. Such a case enabled a broadside photo to be taken of a driving coach in First TransPennine colours at Stonebridge Park sidings. The photo emphasises the length of these coaches, and was taken from an East Croydon to Watford Junction Southern service.

In its normal territory, 185114 passes Mirfield with a Middlesbrough to Manchester Airport service. Taken in July 2009.

At Colton Junction in May 2016, 185134 leads another unit and is seen working from Manchester Airport to York.

In the new Arriva Northern colours, an unidentified Class 185 works a Manchester Airport to Middlesbrough train, seen just south of Colton Junction in May 2016.

The Voyager units can look quite different from different angles, as illustrated in this and the following photo. Virgin 220020 *Wessex Voyager* passes Bedhampton in March 2003 with a Liverpool to Portsmouth Harbour train, one of the now withdrawn services.

An unidentified Class 220 negotiates the curve at Ash Junction, the site of the former branch to Farnham via Tongham, the track bed of which carries on straight ahead. The train is working from Gatwick Airport to Manchester in March 2003, on another lost service.

The longest run undertaken by a Voyager was this Plymouth to Dundee service, which on this occasion was being worked by Arriva Cross Country 220013. It is seen in June 2010 passing Norton Fitzwarren.

Virgin Super Voyager 221109 passes over the junction with the Romsey line at Redbridge, operating a Bournemouth to Glasgow service in March 2005.

Very much off its normal beaten track, due to track work in the Bristol area, a Class 221 is seen at Berkeley Marsh near Frome in November 2006, working a Derby to Plymouth service.

Major work on the West Coast Main Line at weekends in August 2008, led to Virgin trains being diverted over the Chiltern line. Two pairs of Class 221 Super Voyagers are seen at South Ruislip working services between Birmingham International and Euston. In the foreground, 221144 leads 221111 with an up service, whilst 221143 and another head north.

Power car 221115 *Polmadie Depot* carried logos for Bombardier, and is seen at the rear of a Holyhead to Euston train passing Athersone in April 2011.

In Arriva Cross Country colours, 221126 has just passed Wichnor Junction as it speeds along with a Plymouth to Edinburgh service in July 2009.

Midland Mainline Meridian Class 222008 in 4-car format, passes Wellingborough on a commissioning trip to Bedford in April 2004.

With the town and church in the background, 222013, now enlarged to 5 cars, passes Wellingborough in March 2007, with a Nottingham to St Pancras service.

Now in East Midlands Trains colours, 222012 rushes through Harpenden station with a Sheffield to St Pancras express in September 2012.

East Midlands 7-car 222002 is slowing down for its stop at Chesterfield, whilst operating a Sheffield to St Pancras service in May 2016.

The other user of the Meridian Class 222s is Hull Trains, whose unit numbers are well camouflaged into the background colours. An unidentified set is passing Brookmans Park in August 2008 on its way from its namesake to Kings Cross.

Vivarail's pioneer conversion of LUL D stock, now equipped with a diesel engine, stands on show at Long Marston in 2015. (Ian Walmsley)

Using its 3rd rail DC facility, parcels EMU 325004 leaves Kensington Olympia on its way from Willesden Railnet to Tonbridge in August 2000.

A remarkable sight at Harpenden in August 2003, was the sight of three Class 325 postal units working from Crewe to Willesden Railnet, with 325012 at the rear. What was even more notable was that they were hauled by 47739 with 92012 dead in transit!

325007 leads two more units past South Kenton in October 1999, with a postal service from Crewe to Willesden Railnet.

The environs of Paddington host Heathrow Express EMU 332005 which sits ready to depart for Heathrow Junction in February 1998. This was before the stations at the airport terminals had been constructed.

Bedecked, if that is the word, in Royal Bank of Scotland decals, 332005 is about to leave Paddington for Heathrow in November 2005.

332002 gets up to line speed at Hayes & Harlington in August 2010. It is bound for Paddington, as is the companion Heathrow Express Class 360, which has stopped at the station.

In the combined colours of Northern Rail and West Yorkshire PTE, 333010 stands in Ilkley station awaiting the signal to depart for Leeds in July 2009.

Another Class 333, 333016, pulls into platform 2 at Guiseley with a service from Ilkley to Bradford, also in July 2009.

A pair of Class 334 Juniper EMUs, headed by 334021 stand in Glasgow Central station in August 2007. Both units carry Strathclyde PTE colours. (Ian Francis)

Departing from Edinburgh Waverley in May 2016 for Milngavie, 334024 carries the Scotrail Saltire colour scheme.

The first of the new Crossrail EMUs is seen in V shop at Bombardier's works at Litchurch Lane, Derby, in August 2016. Note that this unit is the first to dispense with the former mandatory yellow front end, enhancing the overall appearance. (Courtesy of Bombardier Transportation))

In temporary Silverlink grey and blue, pending a change of franchise, 350114 leads another Class 350 past Headstone Lane in November 2005, with a Northampton to Euston service.

Still in Silverlink employment, 350117 speeds through Cathiron with a Crewe to Euston train, and will soon apply the brakes for its stop at Rugby. September 2006.

Now in London Midland colours, 350243 passes Cheddington on the down main line, but will be switched to the down slow at Ledburn Junction in the distance. It is working a Euston to Northampton train in May 2009.

The OHE gantries mask the attractive station buildings at Atherstone, where 350114 stops with a Crewe to Euston service in April 2011.

The class 350s operated by TransPennine Express carry a striking colour scheme. One of these units is seen at Wool Oaks Mill near Calthwaite in July 2016, working an Edinburgh to Manchester Airport service.

The Class 357/0 series of Electrostar EMUs carried this attractive green and white colour scheme when first introduced. 357028 is seen leaving West Ham with a Fenchurch Street to Shoeburyness train in August 2000.

White with grey doors was the colour scheme used for the 357/2 units, as shown here on 357205 which is passing the Docklands Light Railway station at Shadwell in January 2002. It is also working to Shoeburyness having just left Fenchurch Street.

Now adorned in c2c blue, 357034 leaves Fenchurch Street for Southend-on-Sea. The photo was taken from the DLR station at Tower Gateway in August 2002.

Unfortunately the sun didn't appear at Chalkwell on this day in June 2010 (so what's new?!). c2c 357212 heads west along the shore on its way from Shoeburyness to Fenchurch Street.

Now operated by National Express, 357006 starts away from Limehouse in July 2010, with a service from Fenchurch Street to Grays.

In First Great Eastern colours, 360115, a 4-car Desiro, raises the dust from newly ballasted track in Shenfield station. The date is April 2004, and the service is from Liverpool Street to Ipswich.

In National Express East Anglia grey and white, 360115 passes under the massive catenary structures at the no longer available site at Pudding Mill Lane, working from Liverpool Street to Clacton in April 2009.

Heathrow Express 360204 stops at Hayes & Harlington with a stopping service from Heathrow Airport to Paddington in August 2010.

On the same day, another Heathrow Express stopping service is seen passing the magnificent structures at the approach to Southall station. Note that these Desiros are 5-car sets.

The new Eurostar sets, class 374, are seen working services to Paris. High speed making set number reading impossible, a St. Pancras International to Paris Nord train is seen on HS1 near Chapel Farm, east of Harrietsham, in August 2016.

Leaving the Lenham loops behind, a Paris Nord to St. Pancras International service is formed of a class 374 set, also seen in August 2016.

As first built with Tightlock couplings and classed 375, Southern 375321 stands in Brighton station in the course of a journey from Seaford to Littlehampton. January 2003.

At a site changed out of recognition by the Coulsdon by-pass, 375337 leads another Class 375 through verdant countryside whilst working a Victoria to Brighton express in May 2003.

Labelled with Connex on the front end, South Eastern 375617 has the road and approaches Otford Junction in October 2002 on an up commissioning trip. A Connex liveried 4VEP creeps behind.

The gradient of the up HS1 line at Cheriton is apparent, under which South Eastern 375809 has emerged with a Charing Cross to Ramsgate service. It is November 2006, and the locos in the sidings have nothing to do.

In 2002, 375610 was decorated for Royal Tunbridge Wells, but has lost its gold band and some of its decals by November 2008, still, however, retaining the non-standard blue doors. Arriving at London Bridge as it used to be, the Electrostar is nearing the end of its journey from Ramsgate to Charing Cross.

Now carrying the later South Eastern colours with blue doors and a black band on the lower body side, 375705 stands in Rochester station with a Charing Cross to Ramsgate/Dover train. September 2010.

Another service to Ramsgate and Dover leaves Waterloo East in August 2012, with The Shard tower dominating the background. The unit is 375607.

A Cannon Street to Dartford service arrives at Greenwich, in the capable hands of 376032, having just crossed the balanced bridge at Deptford Creek in the background. February 2006.

Electrostar 376013 stands in one of the bay platforms at Orpington in April 2010, getting ready to depart for Cannon Street.

376024 starts away from Petts Wood in July 2010, working a stopping service from Orpington to Cannon Street.

Now fitted with Dellner couplings, and re-classified into Class 377, Electrostar 377133 sweeps round the bend through Wandsworth Common station working a Victoria to Littlehampton/Eastbourne service in August 2004.

In the shadow of Arundel and its castle, a pair of Southern Class 377s head south with a Victoria to Chichester service in November 2005.

With a semaphore signal guarding the exit from the station at Bognor Regis, 377323 arrives with a shuttle service from Barnham. April 2006.

A Southampton/Bognor Regis service to Victoria starts away from Redhill station in November 2008. The lead unit is 377108, trailed by 377471.

Commissioned by the Southern franchise, but used by First Group on Thameslink services, 377519 approaches Gatwick Airport whilst working from Bedford to Brighton. The train looks so much better without the meaningless squiggles and dashes that First Group seem to idolise.

In the original 3-car format, Capitalstar 378016 arrives at the old station at Highbury & Islington, before it was transformed with the tracks from Dalston Junction. The train is working from Richmond to Stratford in August 2009.

The classic shot on the London Overground at Hoxton in May 2010, where 378147 rounds the curve into the station, with the City buildings as a backdrop. The train is running from Crystal Palace to Dalston Junction.

Up and down trains pass on the DC lines at Headstone Lane on services between Euston and Watford Junction in July 2010. In the foreground, London Overground 378229, in 4-car format, heads towards London.

Now formed of 5 cars, with the extra car in decorative colours announcing this, 378201 leaves Honor Oak Park with a West Croydon to Highbury & Islington train in September 2015.

At Tottenham Hale in July 2011, NX East Anglia 379026, is travelling from Cambridge to Liverpool Street.

Climbing the bank from Liverpool Street, 379027 passes Bethnal Green with a train to Stansted Airport in September 2015.

Class 380 Desiro EMU 380101 stands in Dunbar station with a train due to depart for Edinburgh in July 2015. (Ian Francis)

In a view rather highlighting the unusual design of the front end, 380107 sits in dappled shadows at Edinburgh Waverley, ready to set out for North Berwick in May 2016.

Also seen at Edinburgh in May 2016, 380114 departs for Ayr.

In the striking red livery, a pair of Class 387s, 387202 at the rear, head into Gatwick Airport with a London Bridge to Three Bridges service in April 2016. A Class 442 runs alongside on the down main line. Shouldn't this have been the colour scheme that London Midland trains would find appropriate?

TSGN 387124 accelerates away from Gatwick Airport towards Horley, where a Southern Class 377 is just arriving. The Class 387 is working a Brighton to Bedford Thameslink service. The Class 387/3s for c2c appear very similar.

Class 387 207 rushes along the Quarry line, south of Coulsdon, working a Three Bridges to Bedford service in August 2016. Note the GTL Express branding.

A pleasing colour combination of 387108 in white and 387203 in red pass Salfords working from Brighton to Bedford in April 2016.

A class 387, destined for the Great Western, passes Atherstone in October 2016, working a return commissioning trip from Crewe to Wembley. The units are 387135 and 387137. Even in full sunshine, the livery hardly appears to be green.

Virgin Class 390 Pendolino 390003 *Virgin Hero* ambles along the down through road at Rugby, working a Euston to Manchester Piccadilly express in June 2008.

Showing the tilt available on the sharper curves, as in this case at Atherstone, another Manchester-bound express is being worked by 390037 *Virgin Difference* (what a peculiar name!), in August 2011.

A few Class 390s have carried non-standard liveries. This version advertising Alstom Pendolino stands out on 390004, seen at Headstone Lane in April 2011, working a Manchester Piccadilly to Euston express.

A South East Trains Class 395 Javelin noses its way into Gravesend station in April 2010, having come up from Faversham. Due to OHE failures on HS1, it terminates here. The unit number is 395017.

Having gone ECS towards Ebbsfleet to run round, 395013 returns to form a service back to Faversham. This view shows the old station layout.

Javelins are regular users of HS1. 395025 is seen at Sandway, running at full 140 mph maximum speed, as it works from St Pancras to Margate in full sunshine in September 2010.

395003 rounds the bend into Rochester station, working a South East Trains service from St Pancras to Faversham in September 2010.

South West Trains 444013, led by 444025 depart from Waterloo with a semi-fast service to Haslemere in May 2004.

444014 negotiates Sheet level crossing, north of Petersfield, working its way from Portsmouth Harbour to Waterloo in March 2005.

Near Wimbledon West Junction, 444027 heads towards Waterloo with an up service from Poole, whilst a Class 442 heads west in July 2004. Why, oh why, did SWT get rid of the superb 5WES units?

444004 slows down for its stop at Eastleigh, working a semi-fast service from Southampton to Waterloo. A Class 67 waits for the road to exit the shed lines. August 2005.

A pair of Class 444s zoom up the main line, passing Potbridge in April 2016, with an express from Weymouth to Waterloo.

A pair of SWT Class 450s, with 450055 leading 450071, make their way gingerly along platform 8 at Clapham Junction in July 2004. The train is from Alton, bound for Waterloo.

With a high-rise block in Twickenham on the skyline, 450116 approaches St Margarets in August 2007, with a Chiswick to Waterloo train.

Standard fare on the Basingstoke to Waterloo services is the Class 450. Seen departing Farnborough Main in April 2009, 450012 trails 450115.

An unexpected visitor at Winchfield in January 2009, was high capacity unit 450568, working from Waterloo to Basingstoke. Note that it is numbered in a sub-series 450/5.

Class 458 8029 exits Barnes Bridge with a Reading to Waterloo service, whilst another of the class works the opposite way. August 2004.

Another Reading to Waterloo service is seen at the attractive station at Barnes in March 2003. Note the exotic chimneys on the station building. The lead unit is Class 458 8025.

Unit 8025 takes the LSWR route as it leaves Wokingham in August 2003, with yet a third Reading to Waterloo train. The somewhat unattractive front end has now been replaced on the 5-car units.

The new 5-car Class 458 sets are demonstrated here at Barnes as 458525 heads away to Waterloo with a Hounslow Loop service in September 2015. The new Alstom cab has similarities to those on the Siemens Class 444s and 450s.

A Gatwick Express Class 460 is seen on the old South Eastern tracks at Coulsdon, working an up service to Victoria in May 2002. The unit is number 460007. The white lettering on the roof says Gatwick Express.

Heading down the normal Brighton line at Coulsdon, 460001 passes on its way to Gatwick Airport from Victoria on the same morning.

460007 is seen again with an up service, this time at Clapham Junction in May 2001.

The Class 460s carried advertisements for several airlines that flew out of Gatwick. Carrying logos for Delta Airlines, 460007 passes Earlswood with a Victoria-bound service, hopefully obeying the 40 mph speed restriction. January 2007.

The driving baggage cars on the Class 460s looked like pseudo locomotives, and had bodysides very suited to advertisements. Heading away from Gatwick Airport for Victoria, 460003 carries logos for China on behalf of Emirates Airline. October 2009.

700110 passes Salfords in April 2016, with a test run from Bedford to Three Bridges. The Southern Class 377 would get in the way at the crucial moment!

One of the Thameslink Desiro City units, 700110, heads towards Blackfriars with a driver training run from Brighton in August 2016. It is seen just south of Coulsdon.

South West Trains 707006 stands in the sun at Innotrans in Berlin. September 2016 (Colin Marsden)

Virgin East Coast's 800101 passes Ealing Broadway in May 2016, working from Old Dalby to North Pole, but having to reverse direction at Southall to gain entry to the depot. (Ian Francis)

The first class 800 to carry GWR green undertook a presentation run from Reading to Paddington in June 2016. 800004 stands in the terminus, with the modern design contrasting nicely with the old station clock. (Ian Francis)

Railtrack MPV DR 98956 gives the rails of the up relief line at Luton Airport Parkway some treatment in November 2002.

A very clean MPV trundles along the Reading to Basingstoke line near Silchester in August 2009. Note the label for Network Rail covering the old Railtrack name.

MPV 98928 does a spot of weed killing near Churchdown in October 2010. This unit also has a Network Rail label.

The Eurailscout 2-car unit passes Potbridge in July 2006 on its way from Willesden to Eastleigh.

The Eurailscout speeds along the down main line at Salfords in December 2008, the destination being unknown. A Southern Class 377 heads towards Redhill.